A Poet's Portfolio

Elizabeth Martina Bishop

ISBN-13: 978-1502846730

BISAC: Education & Reference > Reference >
Bibliographies & Indexes

Design by Artline Graphics, Sedona AZ, USA
www.artline-graphics.com

ElizabethMartinaBishop.com.

A Poet's Portfolio

Elizabeth Martina Bishop

Elizabeth Martina Bishop

An Interview by Steven R. A. Johnson

Elizabeth Martina Bishop (l) with her Mentor Cleo Tomer

After looking into your biography I am aware that you have been involved in the arts since an early age. You studied ballet, mime, character and folkloric dance at Balanchine's School of American Ballet in New York City. How have these disciplines informed your current practice of poetics?

Poetry is a way of defining life, a quotidian and every day way of life. It is like performing in an aerial ballet, or reviewing the features of a high-wire act. You are challenged at every turn you take by different forms. Poetry is also a way of testing yourself: in the way of sky-diving, wave-surfing, wind-surfing. But none of these activities do I perform.

The most important thing is that my poetic life began when I was at The School of American Ballet and studying to become a baby ballerina. I attended many sessions at the St. Marks Church-in-the-Bowery at that time and was always inspired by the musical aspect of the dance and how poetry could be set to music.

Poetry takes a form that, when read, may work out in a different way on the page. The way the poem sits on the page is less important to me than they way a poem is read. I am very aware of the musical element in poetry and I'm interested in how musical poetry can get without turning into a song or a lyric. I enjoy putting verse to music and am experimenting with that just now. It seems to me that "chanting" poetry is necessary to get across its semiotics, its symbolic meaning and its posture. Poetry has a physicality that is a mystery. I try to embody my verse in a gesture in an aside while I am reading the wall and performing poetry in the air.

How are you personally inspired by poetry?

What inspires me probably inspires everyone else to act in somewhat the same way. I act on the dictates of my imagination. This fact means I spent a lot of time at night getting up and writing. This is the time when the muse tends to hit with a vengeance.

At other times, when I sit down, I have no idea what I'm going to write. My mind is a total blank. That being said, I think an image eventually floats in and makes its presence known. During my entire life, I have thought poetry came from something that was overheard during the day or from eating something like post-toasties that would take your breath away or make you want to bivouac upon the confines and unknown regions of some unlettered, foreign shore. Today, I am not so certain about all of this, though I think indigestion probably does have something to do with writing poetry. If there is another being living inside of me, I do not know of it, nor of its predilection, for multiple voices are usually given off in the fervent energy embodied in the leaves that in surrendering yield us so much oxygen—whey they're not uprooted!

Would you say more about the feeling of these beings, or multiple voices, inside of you?

Yes, I feel a poem kind of waiting in the wings. It is as if there were a dancer waiting in the wings and eagerly awaiting to go onstage and do a number. Or, maybe she is nervous, I just don't know. I don't know whether these diaphanous spirit dancers are spirits or not. It is as if they are waiting for me to put words that go with their actions on the stage. It's kind of the same thing that a sportscaster does—when they describe the machinations of football players or the moves improved upon by seasoned jockeys convened in the makings of a horse race. If you dwell in the land of metaphors, you live in the world of horse races each day. I feel strongly that poetry must be written only under the influence of waking or non-waking spirits. I feel strongly about this, I am not talking about other kinds of spirits.

Other kinds of spirits?

Poetry is an activity that is all encompassing, at least for me. It appears to me to be an act of translating or transmuting energies, unseen, felt and un-felt. Going from one realm to another, I am aware of being nurtured by certain energies. Often I know of the existence of these energies but I may not be aware of the form they take.

There is a call to becoming a poet that is difficult to revoke or shy away from. It has nothing to do with anything but brain chemistry, so we are told. But the only brain chemistry I have ever felt has been disseminated over every molecule in my body. It is feeling of being a poet, or a painter of words, down to my fingertips. I cannot explain it. I cannot analyze it. But only send the force of energy into the winking eyes of the bardo when the time comes for the cosmic bread crumb to succumb to its natal estate, its place of origin.

I hear you saying that poetry is a calling, maybe your mission embodied. Do you believe that your poetry can change the way people live in the world?

In some ways, I always thought poetry was a self-indulgence. Something people do when they are preoccupied but not really engaged in saving the planet. In my elder years, however, I feel that I can only do what I gotta do, or that which I can do. I am not sure I could run a marathon, but perhaps I could walk a marathon! As for poetry, it is my way of responding to what I see in the world, to make a balance out of imbalance or to improvise ways of looking at the world. It is my way of evoking spirit. It is what I love to do, my passion.

It is also a way of integrating "herstory" and as well as history. On the most mundane level, writing a poem a day is the same as doing a crossword puzzle, but I cannot cope with the labor involved in crosswords.

So then, how do you see yourself in the extended poetic community? How do you place yourself in the lineage, or "herstory", as she is unfolding?

As for influences that have informed my work, there are the Pre-Raphaelite and Impressionist painters – August John and Maxwell Parrish. And the Dutch painters of the seventeenth century are a great source of inspiration—as well as Kandinsky, Mirot and others. I like to think of poetry as a photograph or an old phonograph record. Remember those old RCA Victor recordings?

Not really...

I think of poetry as an old-fashioned art.

Who are the more contemporary poets with whom you've had the pleasure to study?

I have taken poetry classes with many fabulous poets: Mark Doty, David Wojahn, Pattiann Rogers, Jack Meyers, Denise Levertov, Louise Bogan, Muriel Rukeyser, Kathleen Raine, Anne Waldman, Anselm Hollo, Andrew Schelling, Jack Collom, Eleni Sikelianos, and many others.

What are you writing now?

Currently, I have created forty books, seven CD's with music and poetry, and I am still performing recitals on my poems on request. I am also making poetry videos featuring music, voice, and poetry. I am very lazy and don't write poetry unless I get inspired. Three MFA's later, I am looking for another MFA to keep me going!

Any concluding remarks you would like to make, regarding your calling, perhaps?

Poetry is a very healing occupation. I enjoy spending all my spare time trying to improve my style, my voice, and my diction. I am not particularly intellectual, but I love analyzing poetry too and reading other poets to see how they approach the world. To me poetry represents a way of living a good life and it instructs one in finding a way to live. It is inspirational!

Steven R. A. Johnson is writer, translator, curator and publisher (at) Wild Turkey Press. He met the poet and her mentor, Cleo, in a cafe, or bardo, during his undergraduate days at Naropa in Boulder, CO. The poet's first words to him were, "I've been looking for you. I need a typist." And thus was Steven's first lesson in poetry: sincerity in spontaneity.

"The cut worm forgives the plow." - William Blake

Steven R. A. Johnson
Twitter @WildTurkeyPress

THE BOOKS

Feathers in the Wind

Feathers in the Wind represents a compilation of interrelated themes reflected in indigenous inspired portraits, both lyric and pastoral.

It evidences the author's deep connection to the mystical aspects of nature and her continuing dedication to the traditional craft of poetry.

ISBN-13: 978-1461030874 • ISBN-10: 1461030870 • $9.95
Available through Amazon.com

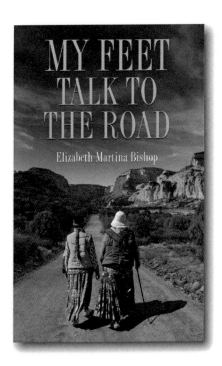

My Feet Talk to the Road

Traveller culture projects masks involving multiple scenarios.
The way of the road may never disappear. The way of the
settled folk continues to change. With the disappearance of
many itinerant crafts today is born a new integration honoring
the old crafts.

These days, we can nevertheless appreciate time-honored
traditions that invite readers to enter a transcendent dream
time. Such an invitation is always present for those who risk a
continuous pilgrimage. That is the fearless way of the traveling
people.

see review on page 150

ISBN-13: 978-1461129646 • ISBN-10: 1461129648 • $14.95
Available through Amazon.com

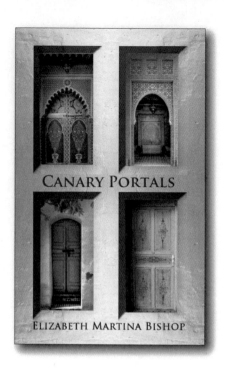

Canary Portals

Canaries have symbolized the healing properties of the sun. Many folk cultures feature the canary as a Rosicrucian dream image showing the canary hovering above a rose.

In this narrative poem the canary operates as a fixture, a landmark, leading the dreamer in a journey celebrating life, birth and death

ISBN-13: 978-1499572117 • ISBN-10: 1499572115 • $9.95
Available through Amazon.com

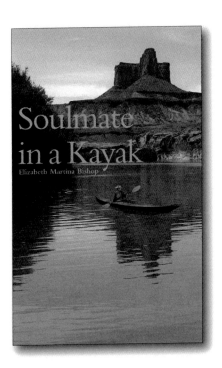

Soulmate in a Kayak

Vignette 1: Soulmate in a Kayak - This section depicts a surreal treatment of a fictitious want ad and the fallout thereof.

Vignette 2: Dervish in a Kiosk - The poems deconstruct the want ad.

Vignette 3: Reinventing Atlantis - Ishi poses questions for those living in so-called civilized society: how can we honor what we don't know we have lost.

Vignette 4: The Green Knight - A pseudo medieval melodrama involving a lovelorn swain who suffers and endures the worst case scenario in a love tryst gone wrong.

see review on page 151

ISBN-13: 978-1461154921 • ISBN-10: 1461154928 • $19.95
Available through Amazon.com

The Awakening of the Anima

No more will I give dreams away,
Except with these more open softer hands,
Than lean down to blow
A thousand sparks into a frozen fire In any case,
I tell you this about my story,
I will not be shut out,
That is quite true
But who will break the glass apart
When love comes through?

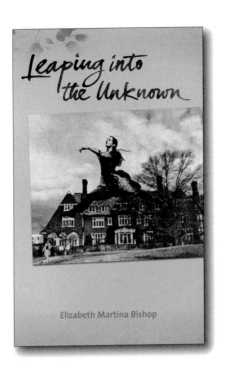

Leaping into the Unknown

A woman reflects on the meaning of life
and turns the sheepfold into a museum,
a sunken garden, and a palimpsest
of poetry and art.

ISBN-13: 978-1463741334 • ISBN-10: 1463741332 • $19.95
Available through Amazon.com

Elizabeth Martina Bishop

Malvinia's Wedding

A folkloric portrait of a woman waiting by various gates for her beloved who may never arrive.

The locations depicted in the text are considered in a visionary and fictional manner.

Part dream, part reverie the quilt of stories supports tribal voices heard in the region of Moorish Spain.

ISBN-13: 978-1475161427 • ISBN-10: 1475161425 • $19.95
Available through Amazon.com

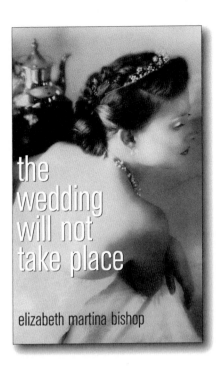

The Wedding Will Not Take Place

This poetic novel promises an occasion for celebration and ceremony. Meanwhile, the ritual of ceremony exists only within the mind of the celebrants who are on the point of undertaking a long journey. This novel promises an ambitious time line involving the completion of a journey. However, no actual ritual of ceremony is actually performed. Instead, the act of writing is seen as a self-redemptive and self-revelatory journey occasioning a spiritual awakening. In the spirit of "Waiting for Godot," celebrants and attendants engage in long journeys of pilgrimage, ultimately leading them towards an inner heart-centered labyrinth. A novel approach to writing a novel without an apparent ending or beginning, words in themselves represent an exploration of the psyches of those who would prepare for a centered afterlife of joy and renunciation.

ISBN-13: 978-1475161205 • ISBN-10: 1475161204 • $18.95
Available through Amazon.com

What is the Function of Moonlight?

What is the function of moonlight? And the high winds? What are they to you? The labyrinth of waves cannot bring reconciliation. The journey has been long and arduous.

A player-piano exists in the waves. Do you exist in a dark calliope of sound? As a new bride receiving a veil, will you take the wheel and steer against the veiled song of the wind echoing?

Steer and know you will not fail. In the clouds are the spirits of your relatives, the spirits of the water, and those that guide you. You are the blue lotus blossom of my awakening. There is order in the meaning of the universe that glistens and stirs in rooms of the ocean.

Poem 31

Forgive me, said the tenor and continued walking away in a very rapid gait that gave him away. How did I know life would be too difficult for me? My dowsing wand could never be used to bend the river of merciful waterfalls of emotion and despair. Is it I enjoy revelry too much? How I long to return the ocean where dragons are crouching and then watch their drowning and only pretend not to see the future, now an unwholesome past.

Wind Rushing Through a Nest of Stars

A delectable award-winning study of poetry that will arouse the sleeping palette of connoisseurs.

A wine-tasting array of poetry that shifts our focus to environmental causes.

Poems with emotional clout bring us to a deeper sense of awareness.

We awake from our sleep with poetry and well crafted poems singing before we take on the day.

see review on page 150

ISBN-13: 978-1475182835 • ISBN-10: 147518283X • $14.95
Available through Amazon.com

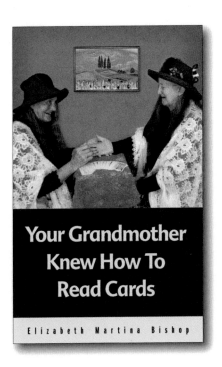

Your Grandmother Knew How To Read Cards

Elizabeth Martina Bishop

Your Grandmother Knew How To Read Cards

From time immemorial, grandmothers have been in the know about the occult arts.

They also know how to read palms. Some of them even write poetry that will make you laugh.

ISBN-13: 978-1479132232 • ISBN-10: 1479132233 • $9.95
Available through Amazon.com

Liverpool Journey

There was this one time I took off on the roads; I hadn't told anyone where I was heading for, Dublin town or the likes of Mullinger. Before too long didn't I find myself on board a steamer bound to Liverpool.

And didn't the likes of the captain take on because of a dreadful storm at sea. Soon enough, didn't the ship begin rolling topsy-turvy on the sea. I felt like a class of a couple of dancing bears performing in a circus of lies.

And didn't the storm take a turn for the worst and water began coaxing itself from the ocean into the portholes. Like as if a blizzard of water was drawn from the thick of winter. You could almost taste the salt coming under your tongue.

Didn't this sailor with a sailor's cap on him come up to me and tell me to take off my cap and start singing the National Anthem of England.

Didn't I tell him I would lifer give my soul away to the devil himself than sing to the Blessed Crown of England.

I swore him up and down and he cocked his head at me and told me that I was a traitor to his majesty.

I told him no one can put it to mind where we

travelers come from: Egypt, India, Pakistan and even the land of Shakespeare took us down since Cromwell's scholar took a dislike to our kind.

Didn't this sailor throw me a few good clouts. There were several scholars on board ship that time and I watched him sweep the water that came in the portholes and still he was cussing me and didn't he take the broom to me and try to push me out of the porthole into the blathering welter of water.

Still and all, the poor ship was rolling but it did not go down. All the deck of cards was falling on the floor and near everyone was screaming for more of Dr. Guinness. I asked the captain: is this boat going straight to the bottom of the world in South Africa?

The captain told me it was a rough crossing. They'd burned all the coal from this side of County Meath to Dun Loghaire. They'd run out of fuel half way across. I expected to be drowned that time. But the other side of land came up out of the sea. Weren't we all grateful to be saved? I tied myself to one of them poles that time and held on to the card tables that were stuck onto the dance floor.

And didn't the Blessed Sister of Charity from Kildare pray for us that night, and don't you know we might be cursed by everyone but that ship never went down.

When I got to Liverpool, I thanked the Blessed Virgin for the tinker's cursed life and I traveled continually all the way to Scotland to pull some tatters and turnips from Stirling. That's what I did. I picked up a queer few bob from that bargain crossing so I did.

Carillon Players and
Night Watchmen

These poems celebrate an abandoned culture of relationship
and an industry based on handcrafts. A cross between the
melancholia of a lost way of life and contemporary media
driven culture.

Between the old world of wandering minstrels, Indian warriors,
and a new world in which technology is often the new poetry

ISBN-13: 978-1480271425 • ISBN-10: 148027142X • $9.95
Available through Amazon.com

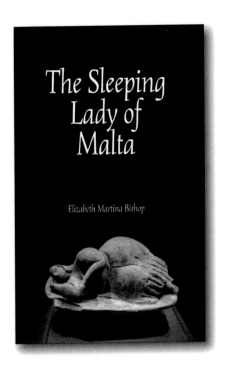

The Sleeping Lady of Malta

An archeological gem, The Sleeping Lady of Malta explores relationship between human, animal and nature and the mystery that no one single poem can evoke.

Native American images predominate because they are cloaked with formidable shadows.

This collection offers a credo as to why I write poetry.
To experience banner moments of consciousness wherein aesthetics and a love of word smithing is born.

The quest for self-knowledge and self-revelation takes nature as its meditation.

ISBN-13: 978-1481946421 • ISBN-10: 1481946420 • $9.95
Available through Amazon.com

Floating World

Poetic excursions and aesthetic exercises that demonstrate the power of the word. The journey readers take will show them unique pathways through often oblique patterns and designs.

Experimental in nature, these poems push the envelope of time and space and express gratitude for the spiritual.

ISBN-13: 978-1482613186 • ISBN-10: 1482613182 • $9.95
Available through Amazon.com

And Then I Heard Them Singing

For poets, the culture of every day life involves engagement and interaction implicit in her ongoing conversation.

A conversation with creatures of the natural world.

These poems offer whimsical and often comical glimpses into old age, thoughts about the afterlife, and the daily karma of survival.

ISBN-13: 978-1482762853 • ISBN-10: 1482762854 • $9.95
Available through Amazon.com

Wings

Birds that touch you briefly then are gone.
The seasons burn under foot.
Heart songs have forgotten numbered cadences,
Sequences, canticles, cantatas

Tears, long forgotten; tears of longing for the ones departed.
Ants lick up all the honey
Left on ragged branches of earth's suffering.
Just–who–you–think–you–are, the illusion of personality

Demands a large piece of clothing
That no longer fits
Breath is about breath enfolding
The wing–harem of your body.
Because of this card, thawed waves breaking on the shore

Almost reverse direction
At my feet, unasked, love holds an empty cup
The dream of music almost deafening.
Skip–your–exercise–as–you–will–
Home–study–improvement–course

You primp before a mirror as a sorcerer, a charlatan
Forgetting how much snow has fallen on the Squaw Peaks

Glimpsed outside the back window
From the first,
I've kept my escape route options open and clear

I want to forget about this mother-daughter affair
Wild bird chick,
I want to put you out to pasture and forget you
Even a boatman, oar-less and drifting
Would learn to swim freely
From you subterranean room of air.

The volcanic ash of Princess Pele changes recklessly
Who-knows-you-as-you-are
A scribe of wilderness and fire, self going up
Against the self in a portrait less probable than air.

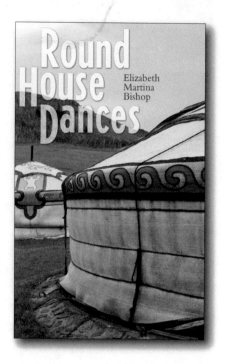

Round House Dances

Round House Dances gifts readers with glimpses into the worlds of the bee shaman, views of the natural world in Ireland and in Boulder, as well as additional encounters with teachers and students.

Everyday experiences surrender readers with poetic vignettes, philosophical, scintillating, meditative, and reflective.

A must read for those who seek heart-centered poetry.

ISBN-13: 978-1482763331 • ISBN-10: 1482763338 • $9.99
Available through Amazon.com

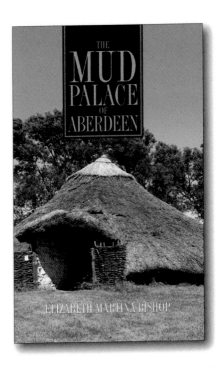

The Mud Palace of Aberdeen

Here are cogent poems that ask questions. Questions that cannot necessarily be answered. Or poetic explorations of parallel worlds. Explorations into unknown and uncharted territory. A whirlwind tour of Native American shamanism. Or just plain shamanism.

The price of being a poet is to create unexplained patchwork quilts in response to the more mysterious aspects of the world around us. Come and enjoy and savor the poetic experience as rich as a good cup of coffee savored in the universal cafe, scintillating, meditative, and reflective.

see review on page 153

ISBN-13: 978-1484926918 • ISBN-10: 1484926919 • $9.95
Available through Amazon.com

Pavlova Awakening

Heavily influenced by traditional narratives, these story poems carry seeds of cosmic consciousness imbued with a dash of La Fontaine, Aesop and Native American Shamanism.

Did Pavlova's awakening to her karmic dance have anything to do with this?

Read these poetic vignettes and you will find out.

ISBN-13: 978-1489522931 • ISBN-10: 148952293X • $14.95
Available through Amazon.com

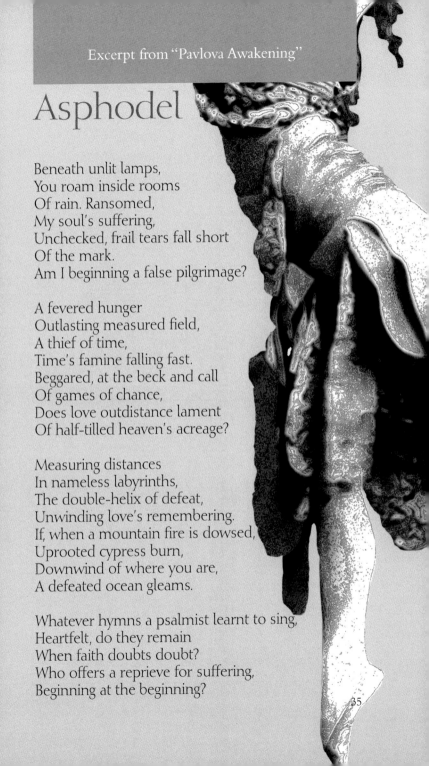

Asphodel

Beneath unlit lamps,
You roam inside rooms
Of rain. Ransomed,
My soul's suffering,
Unchecked, frail tears fall short
Of the mark.
Am I beginning a false pilgrimage?

A fevered hunger
Outlasting measured field,
A thief of time,
Time's famine falling fast.
Beggared, at the beck and call
Of games of chance,
Does love outdistance lament
Of half-tilled heaven's acreage?

Measuring distances
In nameless labyrinths,
The double-helix of defeat,
Unwinding love's remembering.
If, when a mountain fire is dowsed,
Uprooted cypress burn,
Downwind of where you are,
A defeated ocean gleams.

Whatever hymns a psalmist learnt to sing,
Heartfelt, do they remain
When faith doubts doubt?
Who offers a reprieve for suffering,
Beginning at the beginning?

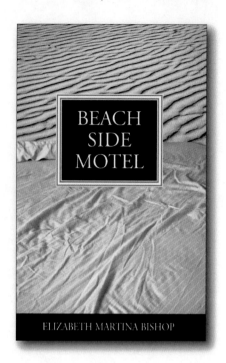

Beach Side Motel

Life sketches reveal inside stories and inner lives of poets who move from place to place.

Each story, each vignette invites a cosmic awareness of paradise on earth.

ISBN-13: 978-1490466736 • ISBN-10: 1490466738 • $9.95
Available through Amazon.com

The Road To Tramore

The Road To Tramore gifts readers with glimpses into visionary worlds, the natural world in Ireland and in Boulder, as well as additional encounters with teachers and students who can unexpectedly appear everywhere.

Everyday experiences surrender readers with poetic vignettes, philosophical, scintillating, meditative, and reflective.

ISBN-13: 978-1490538716 • ISBN-10: 1490538712 • $17.95
Available through Amazon.com

Betrayal

We are going to meet at the beach. I know it, I can feel it
So I go to a trendy dress shop,
Filled with the most trendy gypsy clothes
I can imagine. I want to sink my teeth into a new dress because
My lover will be meeting my later this afternoon at four o'clock.
I want to look scintillatingly beautiful for him.

I told the shop owner "I know it, he's gonna propose to me today
After fourteen years of waiting. Haven't you got a red dress?"
She says, don't you know red dresses are for funerals?
What do you want a kimono? I look at her and say,
"Surely the second coming is at hand, I don't see why you have
To be so insulting. Can't you see what it's like to have been waiting
For this man for fourteen years in seven different countries?"
Men are not worth it. you might as well be an African with a spear
Running after an ocelot. Shed it.

Before you were born you shed your skin. Now repeal the apple
In honor of your inner form from which you can never escape.
Repeal the apple to discover your inner core.
Then throw the skin over your head and list your teeth
As the only thing left indigenous to your body.

Now I'm meeting him on the rock.
He's sitting on one rock I'm sitting on another
It wasn't supposed to be like this.
Why won't he look at me in my new dress?

The sand is plush.
But he says I have something to tell you.
I get ready for the proposal.
This is the twenty-fifth in one month.
He says: I want to tell you about my daughter
She got a job at the bank.

The Art of Swimming

We had never met at any time before,
Yet, hidden behind my shoulder,
You were standing, watching over,

Preparing to open a camera shutter,
Aiming a camera at my retina.

Widening its vast expanse,
As my pupil went on swimming,
Into a field of shimmering stars,

Already flying overhead did birds
Seize the moment to soar heavenward?

At least, the way I recall the story,
The place where I was standing,
Was Broadway and Fourteenth.
Looking svelte in my new black boots,
Wearing my new suede tan mini-skirt,

As I was standing there, doing nothing,
Perhaps I was thinking of what would happen.
Or, of doing nothing later during the day.
I may have wondered what impact this memory would have
On my digestion,
And the connective threads of my tubal ligature.

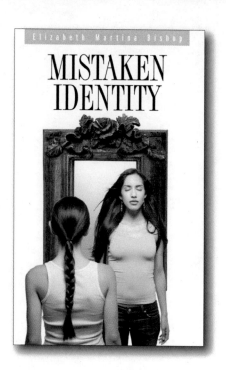

Mistaken Identity

How can you, the reader, awaken to the cosmic dance of poetry?

By savoring the welcome dance of images, visions, and poetic excursions.

Can't afford a cruise? Go on cruise control with this poetry and enjoy the ride. These works will sensitize your awareness so you can soon set sail on the vast sea of improvisation.

Watch as the stirring of your mind, body, and soul will harmonize with a poet's passion for the caress of words.

ISBN-13: 978-1490956305 • ISBN-10: 1490956301 • $12.95
Available through Amazon.com

Black Swan

Roman historians suggested the black swan never existed as a species found in the natural world. However, poets well know the icon of the black swan is alive and well and swimming across many sign posts of pubs in the British Isles.

Read these poems and savor a lyrical exuberance that activates, quickens and celebrates a cosmic song.

see review on page 152

ISBN-13: 978-1491036433 • ISBN-10: 1491036435 • $12.95
Available through Amazon.com

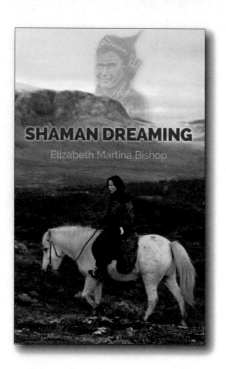

Shaman Dreaming

Shaman Dreaming evokes the spirit of poetry.

When a Shaman dreams she/he usually dreams of an animal to complete a natural healing cycle.

Poetry is a way of summoning animals that have lives that bring readers a sense of spiritual identity.

When you read these poems you may find yourself being grateful you have the freedom to dream in whatever way you wish.

ISBN-13: 978-1491241530 • ISBN-10: 1491241535 • $13.95
Available through Amazon.com

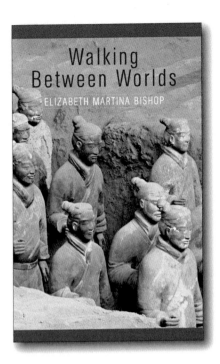

Walking Between Worlds

Beyond the tricks of phenomenological investigation readers may believe the imaginary world of Maya exists.

Poets live in a supernatural arena which is here today and gone tomorrow.

Wordsmithing operates as a way of transcending the limits of the reader's imagination.

An invitation to suspend everyday belief systems continues to invite verbal detours.

ISBN-13: 978-1492223641 • ISBN-10: 1492223646 • $9.95
Available through Amazon.com

Cosmic Parking Ticket

Arrested for watching autumn leaves, a man dreamed he lived inside a poem. Dutifully falling from the sky, birds darted among pine trees. As burnished colors trespassed his body, parking meters kept running. "No such thing as absolute truth," he said.

Although he surmised the fines would be extraordinary, he wondered, could his offense be any more mysterious? In a stillness almost disquieting, he returned to an earlier season. The love of sanctuary, his heart's inner core. "My address has never changed," he thought. "Of this I am certain." In the dress rehearsal of his dream, he recalled forsythia blooming ever so brightly in her hair. The sky seared blue above him in the Caucasus Region. "Girl-friend, why did you abandon me?"

Once the man reviewed every word between them: leaf, stone, roof, space, foxes began frolicking in imaginary caves. Unanchored, he remained outside her poem. Among penitent leaves, blank foliage of despair. When a black gnat lands on the belly of moon, you know disembodied spirits as wounded messengers become unhinged. What will cause the man to dwell quietly among his own rooms of sunlight?

Revelation

Her writing class at the Black Swan. Sam's wife tells her to create a costume out of the back pages of The Irish Sentinel. She laughs. To disclose the reason why she has vertigo would be to betray the irresistible nature of the sailor.

He visited Naples on her birthday last October. Details. Prenuptial agreements. Such a shyster. Heathen that he was. Unknown at the time, a man fallen prey to lower-chakra vices.

Somehow she feels compelled to review the details of her perilous and purblind tryst. She would now write a traditional poem based on a Provencal line-break. She conjured up pictures of make-believe flames flickering on shiny brown logs.

Interwoven with a host of Celtic dragons, soon to be emptied of its ashes, the hearth lay still and calm. Until the members of her class became entranced with the details of her half-story, she was never satisfied.

Praise Song for the Dab Chick

ELIZABETH MARTINA BISHOP

Praise Song for the Dab Chick

When dab chicks are first set out to pasture they may be resistant to various archetypal states of individuation, and integration.

While surrendering to a gradual blending into nature, including the terraced garden plot, the orchard, the tree as well as underbrush, dab chicks eventually gain strength and learn to lean into the angled brightness of flying. Author Elizabeth Bishop tells us specifically the dab chicks are just excuses for the imagination to enjoy earth's biosphere as well as the transformative voice of nature poetry.

ISBN-13: 978-1492893837 • ISBN-10: 1492893838 • $11.95
Available through Amazon.com

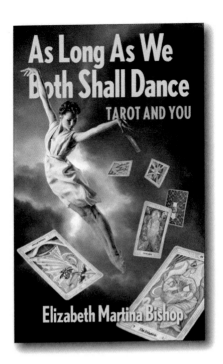

As Long As We Both Shall Dance

Not sure what to do today? Meditate on a Tarot card and find a new sense of direction.

The studies on the Tarot cards offered in the pages of this book may inspire you to make a shamanic excursion into the vast, unknown worlds of poetic endeavor and fantasy.

When using your imagination, the choices you make on the path to self-realization offer new lessons that may later lead you towards a more formal study of the Tarot.

see review on page 153

ISBN-13: 978-1493592722 • ISBN-10: 1493592726 • $14.95
Available through Amazon.com

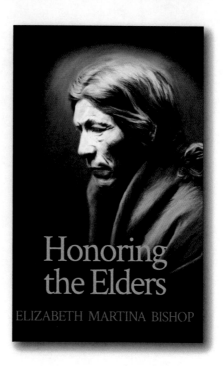

Honoring the Elders
ELIZABETH MARTINA BISHOP

Honoring the Elders

Many of the poems in this collection honor the elders and anticipate the enjoyment of the natural world.

Restoring the importance of Mother Earth and reclaiming her power is central to the premise of this collection of talk stories and poems.

First Peoples were never to be separated from Mother Earth. At the point of colonial contact, the rights of the people were violated.

We are to remember we are all interconnected, no matter what. Much healing and honoring needs be accorded ancestral ways, now and forever.

ISBN-13: 978-14993699261• ISBN-10: 1493699261 • $11.95
Available through Amazon.com

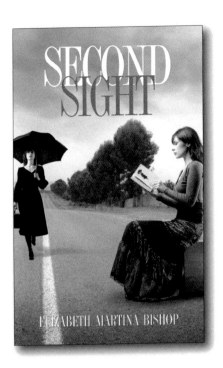

Second Sight

These poems reflect the author's continued engagement with her contemplation of nature and its blessed surround.

Communing with nature is what calls forth a healing poetic response.

The inner paradise of contemplative thought may be the only paradise on earth. Please read these poems aloud and enjoy the metaphorical palette.

ISBN-13: 9781494402129 • ISBN-10: 1494402122 • $9.95
Available through Amazon.com

Blackfoot

Wife, you must not look out of the lodge!
    You that burn sweet grass continually must be
Aware that it is fair on the window of sky
Not to look out at it. See your children are

Secure strapped to the cradleboard. Nothing
Out of the ordinary must imitate the cry of the magpie
In its time. Wife, take care to burn the sweet grass so
Smoke issues up, curls into a wreath that is sweet.

It is morning and I am going up on the prairie
To curl myself behind the branches, behind the bushes
And the rocks. Without eating or drinking, I have adorned
Myself in the very head-dress, the very robe of the buffalo.

It is I who will sing to the buffalo because he is kind.
But, now the people shout
And come from behind to bewilder
The level-headed buffalo. I have come to be afraid for him
I have come to be blind like him.
I have come to know which

Of the herd will wheel around
Letting the hindermost lead them
To the cliff from which two lovers jumped into the crevice.
Pisku piskun! Come make the buffalo filled with light fall
Into the greater light from which they came!

The cliff is not
Disguised as man. Jump into the slats!
Jump into the embrace
Of mountains!
Jump into the dust that sings to your shadows!
Remember the time we were hungry, O buffalo, and could
Not endear you to the edge of the steep cliff?

From us
And our arrows, you ran in safety
Across the valley. Remember
How hungry the people?
No people could topple you.
Remember our maidens, fetching water!
One promised she will marry

If only one buffalo jump into the corral!
One buffalo hears and leaps into the corral like wind.

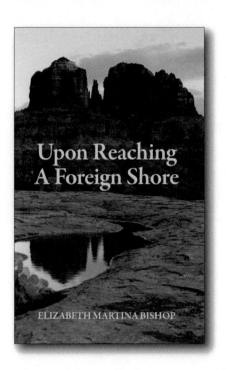

Upon Reaching A Foreign Shore

A sudden leap of consciousness. A leap of faith.
Karma is an open door.

A way of attending to the spiritual nature of the writing
discipline.

This is what poet Elizabeth Martina Bishop is all about.

She leaves the door open for readers to enter into new ways of
thinking about the natural world.

Even within the postmodern urban context, the inner dance
remains the same.

ISBN-13: 978-1494739805 • ISBN-10: 1494739801 • $9.95
Available through Amazon.com

Cosmic Excuse

Poetry contains a recipe within it.
A dash of salt, a dash of wisdom's soul.

These poems reflect the poets' continued interest in nature blended with spiritual insight that makes the listeners' spirit want to dance and celebrate life.

see review on page 152

ISBN-13: 978-1495247651 • ISBN-10: 1495247651 • $9.95
Available through Amazon.com

Camille's Return

Camille's Return consists of a series of short laconic poems about inner and outer transformational states. To remain conscious and acutely aware of the cosmos and all the transcendent changes taking place, poetry can serve as a mediating borderland of consciousness.

Poetry mediates inner realms implicating the shameless mysterious interplay between light and dark. Each poem may be considered a talk story that mesmerizes and leads readers towards the pathway of holistically inspired memoir. Memories of past, present, and future lives are not left out in the cold. Poetry charts the heart's return to grace.

ISBN-13: 978-1496123718 • ISBN-10: 1496123719 • $9.95
Available through Amazon.com

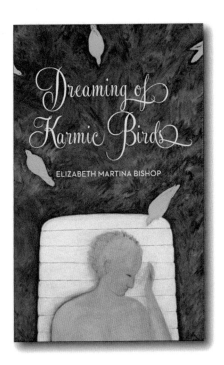

Dreaming of Karmic Birds

The golden birds of karma let us fly free from old constraints and emerge into shimmering sunlight.

Life reviews invoked by the discipline of meditation can lead to new vistas of expanded consciousness and enjoyment of the path of metaphor and poetry.

ISBN-13: 978-1497416093 • ISBN-10: 1497416094 • $13.95
Available through Amazon.com

Leaves

How many leaves have fallen?
If you want to see god
On the battlefield of life,
Be sure to remain sequestered
And somewhat cloistered.

Else agree a darkened cave.
Little torment for a fortnight.
Light may forgive almost everyone,
Even those tongueless hordes
Who can't sing and won't listen.

The wine of unforgiving darkness
Endears everyone with amber honey.
Those who gather around
The wounded won't be seen again
At least, not this century.

Once I saw a horse covered in flies
Super-ensnared in chains he was.
Perhaps, you know who was leading who
To the slaughter house, the house of unrest.
Perhaps, you recall the chanted force

Of a driving desert wind and feckless stars
Bringing sages to an unseen altar of defeat
Before they knew no longer did they need
Stroke their witless beards
Nor falter among the deceit of the living

And now the dead, truly dead.

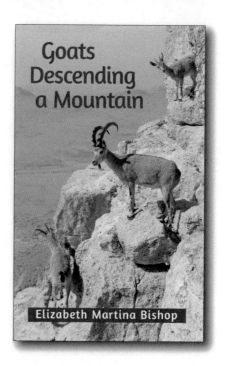

Goats Descending a Mountain

These poems are experimental in form.

Goats Descending a Mountain shows the way in which improvisational forms can ignite mindful steps enabling pathways towards awakening of the imagination, inspiration, and courage.

ISBN-13: 978-1497586512 • ISBN-10: 1497586518 • $9.95
Available through Amazon.com

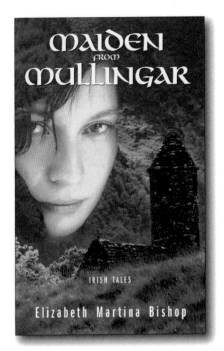

Maiden from Mullingar

The Stories: Irish traveller tales are some of the oldest remnants of traditional oral culture. These stories have been recorded and adapted from original travelers the author met on the roads of rural Ireland. In addition to these tales, this book offers a poetic smorgasbord of Irish culture.

The Background: With the disappearance of many itinerant crafts today is born a new integration honoring the old craft of story telling. These days, we can appreciate time-honored traditions that invite readers to enter a transcendent dreamtime. Such an invitation is always present for those who risk a continuous pilgrimage. That is the fearless way of the traveling people who constantly evoke an old way of life that has been displaced by emigration and industrial development.

ISBN-13: 978-1496123718 • ISBN-10: 1496123719 • $9.95
Available through Amazon.com

Traveller Narrative

God spare us all, what is it you are doing, Nora Lee? Are you starting for to meddle with our souls? Telling your stories outright, those yarns do make us ashamed of being freeborn travelers if not wee but of lonely for the leanest life on the side of the road? And am I killed to death? Aren't my wits well flayed with your canny telling?

Jimmie looked up at Nora as if to throw his hands in the air; then paused and thought the better of it. There was no telling what he would do when she began to tell her stories. He constantly threatened to murder her; in so many words, he was a Canny Lee who rarely failed to examine talk stories from all sides; warring with Nora Lee gave Jimmie a certain kind of satisfaction, but he would never admit it. Still, he had not planned to marry her for her sovereigns nor for her ability to crotchet and to tat lace; meanwhile Nora thought Jimmie a ready slouch and a lush. Here it was teeming with rain spattering on the cobblers outside and she hadn't had time to fetch up a white loaf for tea.

Nora looked at Jimmie and the rest of the travelers gathered in the front room; hers was a face neither bragged nor humbled. With a darting glance that seemed to read the close mist thickening outside the broken window, she began to detail what had gone on in the boarding home the past few years.

"I've been here, what – a year or two?" Nora gesticulated in the air as if momentarily she would recall a float being drawn up to the door and she'd have the context of stepping off the flat cart and walking in the wooden door that with one more person pushing on it would drop its hinges.

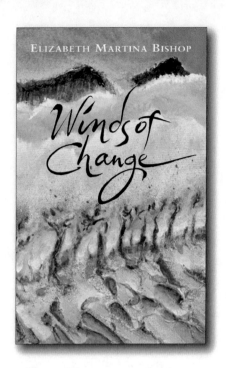

Winds of Change

This collection invites readers to sample new experimental forms of writing by poet, Elizabeth Martina Bishop, author of thirty-five books. Using a metaphysical form of faux memoir, or a memoir based on fantasy and hypothetical realms involved in the human experience, Bishop plumbs the depths of anguish, sorrow, and joy and veers towards science fiction.

She has never written so much prose in her life. She also includes a new diverse collection of poems and a small verse play: Dinner with the Green Tara.

ISBN-13: 978-1499666793 • ISBN-10: 1499666799 • $9.95
Available through Amazon.com

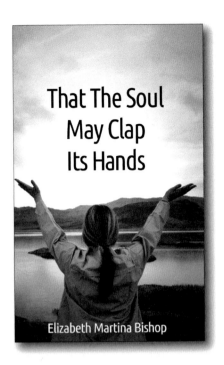

That The Soul May Clap Its Hands

Poetry is a way of life, a way of celebrating many aspects of nature, both dark and light. To celebrate life through poetic exploration is the aim of much Elizabeth Martina Bishop's vibrant work. That being said, poetry can be found everywhere, in ordinary rituals of daily life.

Poetry is a way of meeting the challenges of life as well. Poetry provides ways that aspects of both inner and outer lives may balance and compliment each other. The poetry you find within these pages is not seen as a rarified art form, rather it is seen as a talk story, a way of telling a story that decorates almost all the ample rooms of the heart.

ISBN-13: 978-1500301163 • ISBN-10: 1500301167 • $9.95
Available through Amazon.com

Visionary Waitress

Think of it. The waitress on duty
For ten hours on a swing shift.
Didn't she have a caesarean when she was young?
The knife sits in the flesh among make believe scars.
The spirit of the dead child upon her.
You never get over a thing like that.
A nightgown soaked in blood.
Love grown stale as the last crust
Of bread offered to a dying man,
The one she took care of for a time,
The man dressed in a blood spattered bib.
Cherokee tears shed before what indifferent altar?
Her history is not his history.
Is it the year of the bear or the year of the gnat?
You could make a memory map
Of the entire world with little stick pins in a table mat.
Her feet hurt. Her moccasins worn thin
Beyond the call of duty. It's a no win situation
For the Cherokee Braves. You must be kidding
Not again! Not another loss!
The good red road, almost a forgotten orphan.
Worse than those chancers performing the stomp dance
All the way across Oklahoma in the Trail of Tears,
Her sneakers sweat as if she has never worked for less.
No gold stars pinned on blouses
For princesses of sweat lodges and alms-houses.
Princesses. When she gets home,
She dips her hands in rainwater,
She drinks coffee from a paper cup.

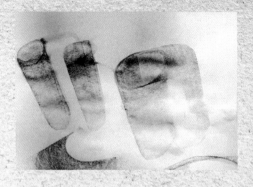

High Rise

We saw a sign on the hotel. They said they wanted to attract new clientele like the twitterers and the googlers. These are in the new buildings and the old buildings. Some have exercise rooms, some have restaurants, some has this, some have that. But they are all purpose buildings like hotels for the workers to live in and have all their needs met. Day care centers etc. New jobs are being created. What happens to the homeless? Great screens are being erected outside the buildings on sidewalks where they used to sleep. The queues for people receiving goof from the Quakers stretches around three blocks. When the steam shovels came, the beds shook in which you slept.

You wondered how can an island support these buildings, what if the electrical grids fail? I recalled a strike in New York when there was no electricity.

My aunt May was alive then and it was difficult then but she only lived on the third floor.

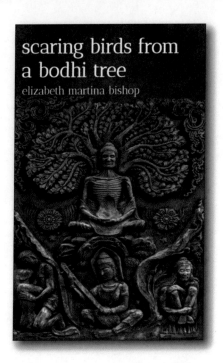

scaring birds from a bodhi tree

Praise and celebration of the changing seasons of nature is the aim of much of poet Elizabeth Martina Bishop's work.

Bringing an intense spiritual awareness to her powers of observation brings readers a delightful experience of what longing for the infinite is all about.

ISBN-13: 978-1500493783 • ISBN-10: 1500493783 • $11.95
Available through Amazon.com

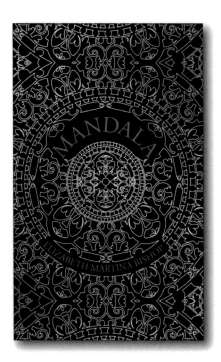

Mandala

Bishop's poems in this volume include multiple projections of dark and light embedded in mirrors operating within the inner realms as transcendent reminders of the possibility of the exploration of body mind and spirit.

Her poems range from transcendent images that spin and astonish with a luminous enjoyment of the senses. It is a kind of slam poetry that is more charming than what one at first thinks of.

It is not easy hallmark card kind of poetry. It invites the reader to love the world of words and allow for the imagination to blossom and explode into rose petals of delight.

ISBN-13: 978-1500526504 • ISBN-10: 1500526509 • $9.95
Available through Amazon.com

Shaman's Lunchtime Cafe

This collection of Bishop's poems demonstrate her Sufi and
Buddhist literary influences as well as her
imaginative interest in transformational states invoked solely by
a classic immersion in nature poetry.

In pursuit of the advancement of her work, she has invoked the
sanctity of the muse and mythic lyrics of traditional lore on
more than one occasion.

She writes a poem a day. Should you desire, you can follow her
onomatopoeic progress on ElizabethMartinaBishop.com.

ISBN-13: 978-1501059933 • ISBN-10: 1501059939 • $9.95
Available through Amazon.com

Meditation

Poetry can be said to be a continuing conversation among pilgrims engaged in the ordered creation of a text.

After each pilgrim's path towards a shrine or an altar, a poem emerges that may appear to out leap the vast amusement of the sun's brilliant light.

No one individual can keep up with nature's interplay of spirits. While some poets may grumble about the nature of the universe, others celebrate the mystery of birth, life, and death and rebirth.

As the reader of this verse, you can decide what to do. So, enjoy.

ISBN-13: 978-1496123718 • ISBN-10: 1496123719 • $9.95
Available through Amazon.com

SOLITUDE

One day in the middle of writing a poem
About the possible sanctity
Of feral cats and their offspring,
When spilling my coffee
Over the entire manuscript,
In the process of climbing
Out of a mindless madness,
I realized, like everything else,
Poetry has its ups and downs.
Once in a torrid landscape
Of blinding light filled with chalices and altars,
While drinking Turkish coffee,
While dreaming of marigolds,
As well as antique lizards crawling
In open fields, I went and asked a client:
So how can I help you today?
When beginning to ask such questions,
When light begins fading away
From almost every card in the Tarot pack,
At such times, I hold myself back.
I keep insisting to myself:
I am not losing my powers.
Though I've climbed out of so many poems
I've created in living room of chic
Literary salons and reviewers housed in the Key West,
Why continue to scale the impossible heights?

THE NIGHT SHIFT WORKER

One evening Max, a night shift-worker,
Lollygagging on the graveyard shift,
Spotted a disc hovering among the hollyhocks.
As Paul, an elder colleague on the same shift,
Began arrowing fish knives at the wall,
Lobsters soon joined in the stage show.
What I want to know, Max asked Paul,
Is it sometimes possible to over-correct
If you're a lobster and crawling out of danger.
Can you somehow absent yourself from
Boiling water and then find a way to dive
Plummeting deep inside a heart-shaped
Aquarium now suddenly filling up with tons
Of aquatic baby eels and fake poinsettias?

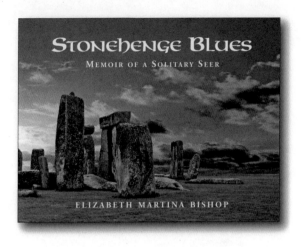

Stonehenge Blues
Memoir of a Solitary Seer

A mysterious and poignant exploration of poetic memoir to deepen an awareness of who we are and where we are headed. In days of uncertainty, how can we find our way?

We can find poetry in an urban coming of age story. How does one interpret life events that seem in old age to have a dream-like quality?

In any event, it is up to each individual to transmute and transform seemingly meaningless happenings. Eventually, we may find out we are wordsmiths who must take the time to witness hidden worlds.   As pilgrims and solitary seers, we can discover our true identities.

see review on page 149

ISBN-13: 978-1502483614 • ISBN-10: 1502483610 • $14.99
Available through Amazon.com

Bravado

The poems in this book represent a further development on the part of the poet, Elizabeth Martina Bishop. She sees intently into the unseen and unspoken words she culls from nature.

While she admits she wants nature to solve every problem and challenge she encounters, of course this remains an impossible paradigm.

If Mother Nature can solve many problems, She cannot dissolve all the problems of life encountered by the mystic seer.

With that being said, can poetry inspire human beings to take care of the planet?

ISBN-13: 978-1496123718 • ISBN-10: 1496123719 • $9.95
Available through Amazon.com

Caravan of Dreams

Caravan of Dreams inhabits the theme of travel, often present in Bishop's work. Bishop uses travel as a way to jumpstart creativity.

Travel in and of itself is nothing unless we travel inward to that pure place of peace instilled with meditation.

ISBN-13: 978-1503275454 • ISBN-10: 1503275450 • $12.99
Available through Amazon.com

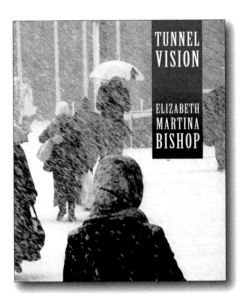

Tunnel Vision

Tunnel Vision expresses a kind of open and reverent supplication before Mother Earth's wintery and windswept altars. Elizabeth Martina Bishop certainly welcomes the chance to spread her wings. Meanwhile, we must try to endure the difficulties of climate change.

If none of us possessed umbrellas, overcoats and central heating, what would we do? So many people succumb to the numbing cold of winter; yet, in extremes of temperature, many may find a kind of a peaceful way of life. Knowing each snowflake is an entirely different jewel may jump start a new story, a new poem.

ISBN-13: 978-1505460551 • ISBN-10: 1505460557 • $10,99
Available through Amazon.com

Silence

Grandmother you never spoke to me before
so until the sunflower was uprooted
no one could see what was coming
or what had been put into the bureau drawer
grandmother, you never spoke to me before
so when the shamans put water
and chicken fertilizer
on the sunflowers I was grateful so I asked
will sunflowers grow from my toes
or from my crown?
And when these tendrils come
will the shamans shout
newly chanted offerings of love?
why didn't I notice no one ever summoned spirit
when I was young? was I to admit
all good things come from heaven above?

HAIKU MOMENT

a chance meeting
in a train station.
a pigeon pecking invisible crumbs
from the waste-basket.
we're sitting waiting
for godot and god's minions
when the pigeon comes
again he bears white feathers
from a darkened place
I suspect from a different shore
the story-teller enjoys her day in court.

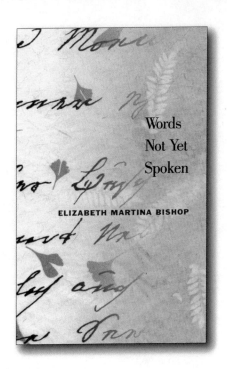

Words Not Yet Spoken

Think of the snow falling.
Think of all the words you've never uttered.
Think of a scarf containing all the colors
Of the rainbow.
Think of a day dream.
Think of nothing.
Is this a poem that as yet remains unwritten?
What is it in human nature that makes one
Want to be a creative artist?
As artists, how do we behold emptiness and silence?
Start from there and then start
Reading the poems in this collection.

ISBN-13: 978-1505863673 • ISBN-10: 1505863678 • $9.95
Available through Amazon.com

French Windows

What holds us together in a unified vision of belonging?
The whisper of a quarrel, the sound of city traffic below, the
sound of chirping birds, all these elements signify a return to
the mystery of the ebb and flow of life.

We celebrate the billowing of bright curtains, shielding us from
seasons of loss and uncertainty, and instead, inviting us to a
future filled with contentment and joy.

ISBN-13: 978-1507554418 • ISBN-10: 1507554419 • $9.95
Available through Amazon.com

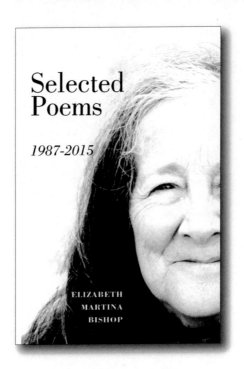

Selected Poems 1987-2015

The poems in this collection represent a distillation of Bishop's works and showcase her sense of humor, as well as her whimsical approach to the art of writing poetry.

While the parameters of her wide ranging poetic style are influenced by 'sound poetry' and her affection for performance art, she stands in favor of the idea that poetry may return us to a spiritual place that invokes a ravishing journey of inner awareness, peace, and soulful contemplation.

see review on page 148

ISBN-13: 978-1507527849 • ISBN-10: 1507527845 • $25.25
Available through Amazon.com

The Goddess Lives
At the Columbus Caffe

These photos and poetry gathered here reflect the creative bridge in communication alternating between meditative image and the power of words.

The life of the bohemian poet is revealed, the aesthetics of image is reproduced for your enjoyment in order to jump start the reader's imagination.

ISBN-13: 978-1511473569 • ISBN-10: 1511473568 • $11.95
Available through Amazon.com

Poet's Angst

Without any sense
Of interrupted journey
I'm looking for some kind of a poet.
If sparrows embolden me, so be it.
I ask whose poem are you?
No answer.
If silence prevails,
Among the hymnals
Held by conformity's muse
If everyone of them
Resigned to singing in a choir loft,
Make me an offer I can't refuse.

So now I'm running through parking lots,
Past houses falling into ruin,
At top speed
I hasten past furrowed fields,
Past abandoned chicken houses of my youth.
For god's sake, where can I find a pen
To affirm a wilderness of speech,
To state my truth, my suffering, and my pain?

breakfast for elders

at the Columbus Cafe
we sit eating pancakes
and drinking orange juice
every morning
and all this is happening
after Columbus
discovered America
so tell me we belong
to some other country than our own
tell me there can be no sweeter
arrangement than this
our books edited for us
and completed before we awaken
and the universe settles
for all of this

The Secret Lives of Poets

This book represents a transformational
approach to the visual arts as well as poetry.

As a collaborative experiment,
both visual arts and poetry
help to bridge the arts and inspire
the development of new poems.

ISBN-13: 978-1512111996 • ISBN-10: 1512111996 • $22.95
Full Color Interior • Available through Amazon.com

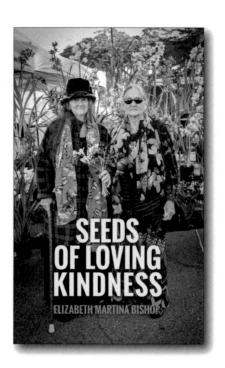

Seeds of Loving Kindness

Reading Elizabeth Martina Bishop's poetry
Is not unlike visiting a flower market
That provides a visual feast.
Poetry is released when in full bloom.
It is here for sale.
For the price of a bouquet of roses.

Choose to buy the flowers or the book.
We don't care, as long as you consider it
An act of loving kindness towards yourself

ISBN-13: 978-1512304596 • ISBN-10: 151230459X • $23.95
Available through Amazon.com

Whoever Comes This Way:
The Sedona Poems

Found art discovered on the sidewalks of San Francisco created the interpretive stand point for this creative work.

Make your own scrapbook out of the flotsam and jetsam of memorabilia and let the intriguing sense of potpourri swirl among the majesty of the red rocks.

ISBN-13: 978-1514856680 • ISBN-10: 1514856689 • $21.95
Full Color Interior • Available through Amazon.com

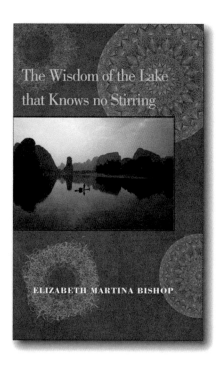

The Wisdom of the Lake
That Knows No Stirring

This collection of poems inspires, educates, and challenges readers to face life's daily vicissitudes and enjoy the journey towards enlightenment whatever way the path unfolds.

Why write poetry?

When you read the poems in this collection, you will get a taste of a poet's palette in a wisdom-filled landscape of the surreal and magical.

ISBN-13: 978-1515257875 • ISBN-10: 1515257878 • $9.95
Available through Amazon.com

french pianist

the French pianist and
her little French daughter
after baseball practice for my brother
my ballet school how I envied the little girl
her tight golden braids curling
into fists of rage
the mother smoking like a chimney
playing Chopin back to back
with Turkish March tunes
or Saint-Saëns *The Swan*
her mother drunk and drowning
as she was on music
loved her child more than any of the students
that's what I noticed
she would have given her life for her
her little girl twirling next to the piano
twirling like a rose

dreams of a mansion

this is what you think you want
a bigger trapeze
a bigger plane
a longer train ride
a bigger luna moth
but in truth
you lament the passing
of your grandmother
and with her went her diary
with all its subliminal messages and commas

Codfish On a Tin Plate

This is the first book penned by poet and author Elizabeth Martina Bishop that features a commentary relating to each of the poems in the text.

In deriving the commentaries, Elizabeth has noted that such prose texts often morph into prose poems that are filled with witticisms and further poetic insights.

In no way are the commentaries supposed to represent a critical evaluation of the aesthetics contained in each poem. The poems in this book are utterly surreal in expression and have as their focus: an invitation to partake of a hearty meal full of poetry, frivolity, and fun..

ISBN-13: 978-1533658586 • ISBN-10: 1533658587 • $9.95
Available through Amazon.com

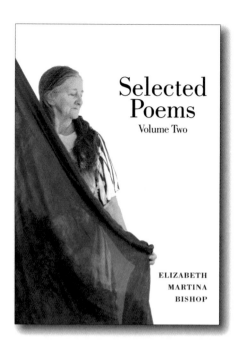

Selected Poems Volume Two

Volume Two of Selected Poems reflects Bishop's diverse and divergent style ranging from heart-rending lyrics to poignant narratives, monologues and plays. Generally her style mirrors the concerns of indigenous people and the mysterious nature of image and metaphor bursting upon the stage of life.

In her work she struggles against the diaspora of time, aging and the ability to restore the strength of remembrance, memoir and epiphany. Without the gift of poetry, we cannot celebrate the soul's astonishment and grace that transforms and shapes the life experience.

ISBN-13: 978-1518826986 • ISBN-10: 15188269895 • $25.00
Available through Amazon.com

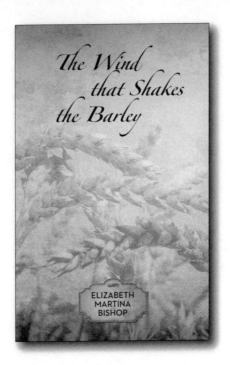

The Wind That Shakes the Barley

This poetic evocation of spirit is part of a controlled semiotics ultimately contrasting with the force of a wind that can suddenly blow through a field, changing everything in an instant. The flowing of the wind of spirit can surrender a harvest consisting of many days or even a few days whereby we can enjoy the sound of the wind and the soughing touch of the wind on the body.

While the wind of spirit may know how to touch us, perhaps we will never understand the density of the soul force doggedly following us all our days, no matter how long or short. In the song of the wind, the poet hears verses that can be gathered up in sheaves later crafted with the constraints of formal verse or let loose in free verse.

ISBN-13: 978-1519778383 • ISBN-10: 1519778384 • $9.95
Available through Amazon.com

La Naissance des Jeux Floreaux
Destiny of Dancing Brides

The poems viewed here suggest an integrated aesthetics indicating poetry persists in multiple forms. Poetry may be seen as a part of our lives lived in harmony and balance. In the old days, when people celebrated the harvest before maypoles and wore floral wreaths, flowers were a constant reminder of nature's abundance.

La Naissance des Jeux Floreaux beckons towards the old days when flowers communicated a heartfelt abundance of messages drawn from metaphysical realms; global warming had not yet become a reality.

ISBN-13: 978-1523881109 • ISBN-10: 1523881100 • $9.95
Available through Amazon.com

First Breath,
Last Breath

I know I've lived before, no kidding.
What should I do to bend the antiphons?
What can I accomplish to do your bidding?
Should I lean on one foot like a wise heron?

What should I do to bend the antiphons?
Whatever the case, harvesting the moment,
Leaning on one foot like a wise heron,
Listen to the message you were sent.

Whatever the case, harvesting the moment,
Glancing at your reflection in a pond,
Do you listen to the message you've been lent
And sanctify the blessings of beyond?

Glancing at your reflection in a pond,
In a parallel life you've pawned for gold,
Why subtract the soul-helmet on loan?
Why not settle for a wand of marigold?

In a parallel life you've pawned for gold,
What can I accomplish to do your bidding?
Why not settle for a sprig of marigold?
I know I've lived before, no kidding.

Seeing Eye to Eye

She waits for a sign
  Perhaps an eaglet
   Will drop a feather
   By a field where
    Flowers already
     Dotting mountains
     In choreography
     Breathing
      Queen Anne's lace
      Of earth's unlit burial
      Outdistancing rooftop
      Buttressing wind
      If rain unpin its stuttering
      And mindless wound
      Whose wordless womb-dance
      Invite suttee
      Unpinned
     From stammering sky
     Wat if the tongue of the world
     Unloose in crippled fire
    As if love widowed

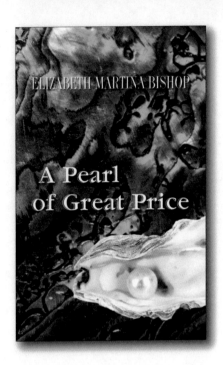

A Pearl of Great Price

Poet and author, Elizabeth Martina Bishop, has fashioned a well-crafted work that demonstrates a provocative and thematic text. The book you now hold in your hand possesses an ambiance indicative of the divine feminine.

Looking at ways of living in the world and approaching new paths that deepen and develop a voice of witness in the wilderness is what this book is all about.

It will open your mind and delight your heart.

ISBN-13: 978-1533345158 • ISBN-10: 1533345155 • $9.95
Available through Amazon.com

She Who Brings the Rain

These poems are about opening doors to new realities experienced by the critical mass of people at the present time.

Against the changing dialectic and synergistic tapestry of history which, like the wind, is always changing, poetry unfolds.

ISBN-13: 978-1530579396 • ISBN-10: 1530579392 • $9.95
Available through Amazon.com

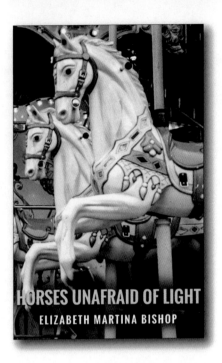

Horses Unafraid of Light

Being unafraid and loving life's challenges is the theme
embodied in these poetic works that are filled with
serendipitous awakenings, transformations, and full moon
meditations.

Those who love the romance of poetry and Hafiz will enjoy
these poems when people can take enough time away from
work to enjoy nature's magical offerings.

ISBN-13: 978-1530932665 • ISBN-10: 1530932661 • $9.95
Available through Amazon.com

Star Gazing

These new poems were all written during the first two months of 2016. Taking the line of least resistance, poet Elizabeth Martina Bishop has penned a series of confessional narratives and lyric poems emphasizing the interpenetration of nature in all things.

Come witness a new body's awakening, the precious eyes of a nighthawk, the beauty of a sunset, the surrendering of self in a daydream.

ISBN-13: 978-1530271849 • ISBN-10: 1530271843 • $9.95
Available through Amazon.com

STAR-GAZING IS FOR THE BIRDS

I keep waiting for a day of judgement.
A pearl of great price seems over-rated.
If lovers and dreamers alike make common cause,
Discomfited by a tidal wave outside the book of life
Thwarted by storms, moon-driven that immutable ocean
Torn by supple clauses of logic's reason.

Why ignore the scattered voices of the mountain?
In presence or absence of light, why pretend
To overcome the eyes of the sleeping dreamer?
Who will redeem those parading dutiful tasks
Unasked, I cannot speak for anyone that's lost.
Into flame and fire of a perfumed wind
Who dares bend the medicine of truth

If no one can extinguish the bravery of the lightening way.
Is it an acrobat from an non-extinguished hearth
Surrendering as he slips from thorn-filled noose
When living apart from love, no longer pretending to exist.
Something else must needs be said
Trapped within a thorn-filled veil,

Before sisters and consorts of a holy well
You have borrowed the clothes of heavenly house.

Owl Harvest

Birds cry out in anguish among fallow fields.
Though this is not the hour for the magnolia and the willow.
I wait. I sit. I wait for old age to bring her scythe.
Before the turning of the harvest beneath the cold light
Of the evening star, thus far a newer demon is birthed
As winter warriors have waited for as much as this
Out of earshot in the desert of yearning for morning.
Though I might wait and linger among verdant hills
Where stillness spooks the bell-tolled hour
Even among most savvy of coyotes and foxes,
My future lulls its gospel music to the inner core
Weaving and spinning an empty stem from a crooked bough,
I feel I've waited long enough. Mantras are exhausted.
Furies have despaired of ever gaining new ground.
Blindly I grope for a vision in an aspen forest
Whose leaves have turned to russet then to gold.
If I must grapple with a deer, a bear, a wolf,
Let the owls spread their wings and be done with me!

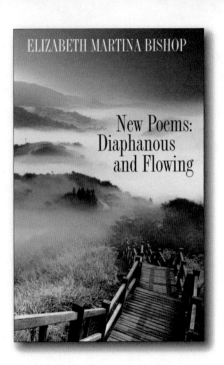

New Poems: Diaphanous and Flowing

Diaphanous and Flowing introduces poems penned by Elizabeth Martina Bishop. The poems translate from supernatural realms into the realms of every day existence.

How should a poet act? Is poetry a practical aspect of a mystical life? Are there aesthetic boundaries between the scientific and the more poetic and intuitive realms?

If so, what happens when a poet transgresses these boundaries? What are the cultural issues that emerge? Is feminism a practical art?

ISBN-13:978-1532964206 • ISBN-10:153296420X • $9.95
Available through Amazon.com

Bear Blessing Salmon

Bear Blessing Salmon is a collection
that details the cycle of life
and nature's hand in it all.

ISBN-13: 978-1537169903 • ISBN-10: 1537169904 • $9.95
Available through Amazon.com

Leaving No Stone Unturned

A short introduction to the poems in this collection delivers a
cogent meditation on the nature of inspiration and the nature
of transformation experience through the expansive activity of
wordsmiths.

Hence, readers can assume perhaps the power of meditative
states encourage readers to follow multiple pathways opening
doors to imaginative realms.

ISBN-13: 978-1534717787 • ISBN-10: 15347177817 • $9.95
Available through Amazon.com

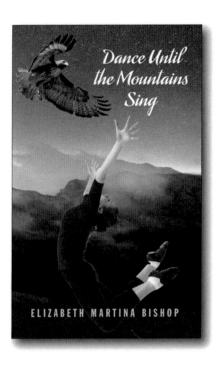

Dance Until the Mountains Sing

These poems were written in the heat of a hot summer when
the author wished to go and celebrate summer by the seaside.
The mountains represent the yearning for higher mind and
lofty spiritual notions that, when are placed within a diminutive
poetic voice, may disappear into thin air.

ISBN-13: 978-1535359207 • ISBN-10: 153535920X • $9.95
Available through Amazon.com

Excerpt from "Dance Until the Mountains Sing"

Night Sky

when you tumble
out of the bedclothes
to watch me dance,
I ask: what is spirituality
does it humble me?

I had to come from somewhere
to understand the bragging
of distances among
stars angling in on the night sky
what it means to surrender
to the avalanche of sound
grandmother, your songs
have entered through my spine
now that you are gone
you have left me alone

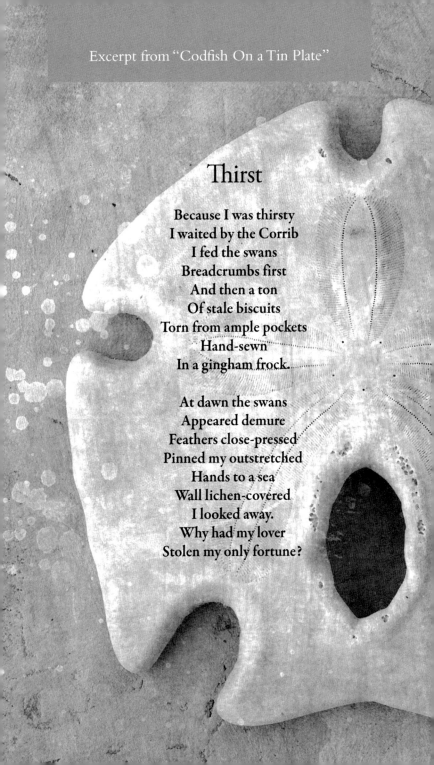

Thirst

Because I was thirsty
I waited by the Corrib
I fed the swans
Breadcrumbs first
And then a ton
Of stale biscuits
Torn from ample pockets
Hand-sewn
In a gingham frock.

At dawn the swans
Appeared demure
Feathers close-pressed
Pinned my outstretched
Hands to a sea
Wall lichen-covered
I looked away.
Why had my lover
Stolen my only fortune?

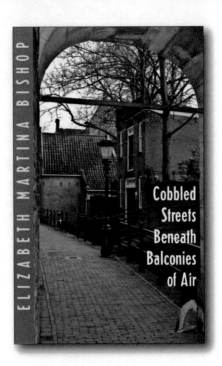

Cobbled Streets
Beneath Balconies of Air

These poems were written during a cold spell. Winter descended and fall suddenly ended. As a reader, you are holding in your hand poems that reflect that post-postpartum feeling reflected in the descent of a sudden cold snap. You can no longer wear a light summer coat. You have to bundle up to stay warm. The tenor of the poems is more intense and some poems are pleading with the goddess for better weather ahead. Instead, storm fronts are moving in and the warm sunshine of Indian summer is a sweet recollection. This book continues the theme begun in The Woman Who Lived on Bird Street. With that theme in mind, poems are a continued source of grounded epistemological inquiries pertaining to inner and outer space, and the poet as artiste in exile in contemporary society.

ISBN-13: 978-1541004122 • ISBN-10: 1541004124 • $9.95
Available through Amazon.com

The Green Knight
From New Mexico

A pseudo-medieval melodrama
involving a lovelorn swain
who suffers and endures
the worst case scenario
in a love tryst gone wrong.

ISBN-13: 978-1537378275 • ISBN-10: 1537378279 • $8.95
Available through Amazon.com

If Ever You Lived Before

Here is a smorgasbord of poetry. The offerings here represent a compendium of old and new works written within the last five years. All are from the inspired works of poet Elizabeth Martina Bishop who has been writing since the age of seven years old.

Many of the poems selected here can lend readers a collage of witness extending the extemporaneous aspects of her works that range from lyric to narrative poems.

Some of the poems deliberately offer lyric panegyrics and pose metaphysical questions that can never be fully answered until a deepening voice develops within the parameters of the next visionary collection.

ISBN-13: 978-1539618317 • ISBN-10: 1539618315 • $16.95
Available through Amazon.com

The Woman Who Lived On Bird Street

A trip to the first Yeats Summer School held in Sligo, Ireland provides the backdrop for a poetic sojourn through magical time and space.

For readers of Bishop's verse this attractive volume will provide new love poems, poems of childhood as well as meditative vignettes on old age.

ISBN-13: 978-1540345080 • ISBN-10: 1540345084 • $9.95
Available through Amazon.com

Lake Champlain

I ride the wind
On Lake Champlain
Mist-ridden the waves
Slow the courteous pace of canoe
Autumn leaves drift down
Landing on water's edge
The world must settle down
Surely the world will do same.
The human race denies
Its unspeakable rage
Nothing slows down
The sacrilege of years
So many things
Better left unsaid.

Painting By Number

Not in my line of credit
Imagine the hotel room
With smoke rings
Lunging off the balcony
And trying then to build
Cacophony of pigeons
With a rubric of despair

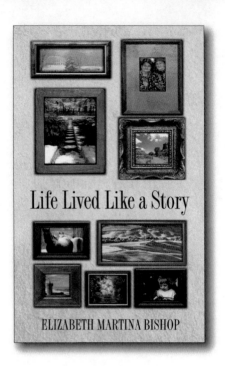

Life Lived Like a Story

These poems by Elizabeth Martina Bishop merge plot-lines of of story poem with the crescendo offered by the lyric narrative.

Each poem has a mystical quality and evidences a search for the ineffable and inexpressible in language fraught with imagery, metaphor and allusion.

This volume contains poems about family, poems about work, and poems about every day existence of an elder living in community with other artists interested in the aesthetics of self-expression and social justice.

ISBN: 9781092633369 • $9.95
Available through Amazon.com

Dance for the Coyote Woman

An Irish librarian called these poems of Elizabeth Martina Bishop: "my kind of talk story..and my kind of poetry." As an Irish librarian, he had come across many books in his life time and now he felt that this was a book worth savoring. Why? He felt that Bishop's work possessed a certain flavor which is full of whimsy, and strange twists and turns that make poetry a ready part of a Celtic inspired story-telling tradition.

These are part of Bishop's interest in the strangely magical world of nature. Her poetry is unpredictable and inspiring in a good way. Read and be inspired! Enjoy and don't be afraid of the wide expanse of the poetic imagination!

ISBN: 978-1546433958 • $15.95
Available through Amazon.com

Arabesque

Arabesque represents a collection of poems of the first order.
The poems are akin to lucid dreaming in that the author
dreams most of her poems while asleep.

The poems contain experimental formats that will intrigue the
eye as well as the ear. These are poems which will astonish,
inspire, and will render readers a lingering sense of gratitude for
the beauty of nature and the music of nature.

ISBN: 9781796221411 • $12.95
Available through Amazon.com

Enough Bird Song to Go Around

This book details some of the meanings behind the individual poems in this new collection. Certain of the thoughts that go into poetic creative output often result in subsequent evocations leading to the birthing of new and original poems. If you do not like poetry because you must decode the literal meaning behind every word, you may enjoy this book as the annotated explanations may shed further light on the mystery of poetry.

Elizabeth did not attempt to translate each poem in a line by line analysis, but rather she wishes to supply some personal details that might illuminate some of the context that led to the writing and craft behind these verses. She compares the process of writing to finding the pearl in an oyster shell. It is her hope that the annotations bring about a clarity and a new sense of vulnerability in compassionate awareness.

ISBN: 9798578628955 • $12.95
Available through Amazon.com

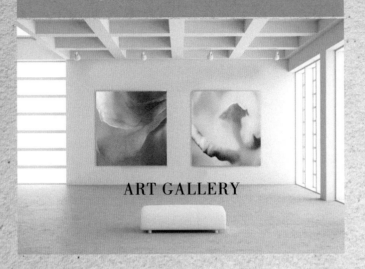

ART GALLERY

Everyone is seeking fame:
A perfect visionary painting of flowers.
Wise women have depicted flowers as a
wealth of posies,
Rare and aromatic.
Flowers as ghosts of a bygone era,
As a lightening flash,
As a mask.
A portrait of a dancer
Adjusting a satin slipper.
The body can appear as libidinous
Or as decrepit as an artifact.
Here, anything is possible.
Feet can be made of satin.
Skin as sallow as a candle flame.
Name your price
Or kidnap a rose.

ORACLE BOOKS

What is an oracle book? These are calendar books whereby you can look up birthdays, weddings, funerals and celebratory dates and see if there is a message contained in the poems. Or, you can use the book as an oracle book and just see what page falls open that will contain a message that seems relevant to your life in some way.Even though these books have dates in them, the dates are adjustable to your personal needs and interests and can be used for events that are significant in your life cycle.

When a Spirit Opens

A companion piece to two other collections *When a Spirit Opens* continues a foray into philosophical discourse. Poet Elizabeth Martina Bishop uses poetry as an excuse to pose impossible questions. We don't expect the reader to answer the questions but merely savor the possibility for the enjoyment of poetry. Delving into the mystery of life which can include birthday celebrations as markers for the life cycle, these poems lend the reader a chance to sit down and relax. Reflecting on the nature of life can sometimes bring about a realization regarding life's many seasons. Why not foster a sense of gratitude for life. When life becomes a flashpoint for improvisational poems, anything can happen. The imagination can grow and a spirit can open like a flower.

ISBN: 9781071244234 • $24.95
Available through Amazon.com

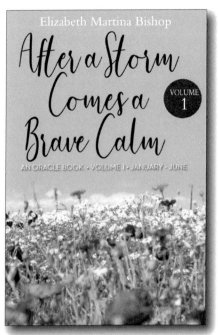

After a Storm Comes a Brave Calm – Volume 1

These oracle poems reflect the interest people have in celebrating the unique messages chosen for particular birthdays. Aside from that, this book can be used as an oracle in order to give you a chance to gaze into the depths of a poem. Two oracle books cover each and every day of the year.

If your birthday poem speaks to you as an oracle poem or speaks to some of your loved ones, so much the better. The entire year is contained in two volumes, so in order to benefit from the inspiration of an entire year's reading, you need to purchase both volumes. This first volume covers from the time period January through June. The second volume covers the period from July to December.

ISBN: 9798638487270 • $19.95
Available through Amazon.com

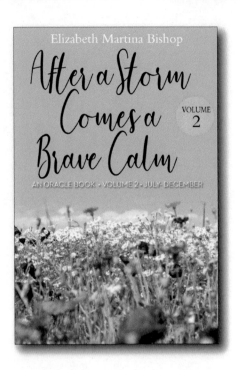

After a Storm Comes
a Brave Calm – Volume 2

These oracle poems reflect the interest people have in celebrating the unique messages chosen for particular birthdays. Aside from that, this book can be used as an oracle in order to give you a chance to gaze into the depths of a poem. Two oracle books cover each and every day of the year.

If your birthday poem speaks to you as an oracle poem or speaks to some of your loved ones, so much the better. The entire year is contained in two volumes, so in order to benefit from the inspiration of an entire year's reading, you need to purchase both volumes. This first volume covered the time period January through June. This second volume covers the period from July to December.

ISBN: ISBN: 9798643860976 • $19.95
Available through Amazon.com

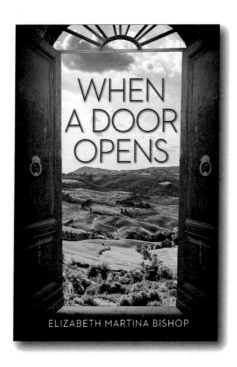

When a Door Opens

A fitting and well-appointed companion volume to Bishop's original birthday book, When a Door Opens surrenders innovative daily offerings that celebrate and review hidden and astonishing aspects of your life.

Here is a golden opportunity to follow hidden pathways as revealed in your particular birthday and the birthdays of friends, relatives, and colleagues. The volume you hold in your hand will allow you to savor the promise of a truly cosmic adventure, the promise of a unique poetic blessing as it unfolds throughout the year.

ISBN: 9781071244234 • $24.95
Available through Amazon.com

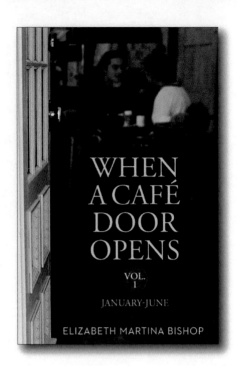

When aCafe Door Opens
Vol 1

If you enter the dream time, you can enter into the realm of poetry. If you dislike poetry, you may miss a birthday poem seen as a suitable container for a message written to embrace any number of occasions worth celebrating.

You can use this calendar book as an inspiring oracle book if you want. If you don't want to, that's all right. I see poetry as a dazzling attempt at self-expression. I see poetry as a daring dance into the realm of sweet and daring words, words that satisfy, comfort, soothe, and heal. You may sing in the shower, meditate, or sing the blues, but take time to read this book: When A Cafe Door Opens.

ISBN: 9781071244234 • $19.95
Available through Amazon.com

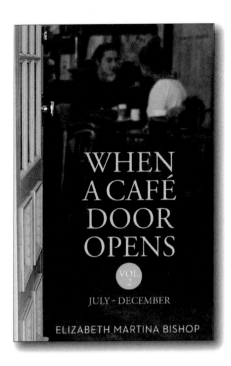

When aCafe Door Opens
Vol 2

If you enter the dream time, you can enter into the realm of poetry. If you dislike poetry, you may miss a birthday poem seen as a suitable container for a message written to embrace any number of occasions worth celebrating.

You can use this calendar book as an inspiring oracle book if you want. If you don't want to, that's all right. I see poetry as a dazzling attempt at self-expression. I see poetry as a daring dance into the realm of sweet and daring words, words that satisfy, comfort, soothe, and heal. You may sing in the shower, meditate, or sing the blues, but take time to read this book: When A Cafe Door Opens.

ISBN: 9798561976759 • $19.95
Available through Amazon.com

House of Words
Sonnets of Change

The work you hold in your hand serves as part of an oracle series by poet Elizabeth Martina Bishop. A carefully crafted sonnet introduces each day of the year included all within the pages of one handy volume. Enjoy a new understanding that proverbs, and pithy fortunes reflect the need for the dynamic presence of birds within the cosmetic aesthetics of the cosmos indicating the creative ethos ensconced within the postmodern context. If you enjoy this book, you may find it an attractive accompaniment to Bishop's Canary Portals.

ISBN: 9798643860976 • $24.95
Available through Amazon.com

When A Window Opens

"Astounding! A shimmering work of such poignant width and breadth. I was captured on page one. The words are rugged and rich and truthful, easily evoking reveries upon this living and vibrant world of which we are all native.

The stories give my soul pause—I am both rested and revived. I see threads of magic woven into all our Earthly guises. .... the aching hopes ... the quandaries ... but, above all, the persevering elegance of our soul's quest. Put this beautiful collection next to your reading chair and bed stand.

It is a labor of love." - Thomas Jacobson

ISBN-10: 1517415772 • $25.00
Available through Amazon.com

Tracking the
Snowshoe Hare

ELIZABETH MARTINA BISHOP

Tracking the Snowshoe Hare

Succumbing to serendipity, many poems are written under the
guise of chance inspiration garnered from unexpected meetings
with others, real or imaginary, Though many people are still
donning colorful masks, meetings still take place. Six feet apart,
people can still practice the art of conversation. Developing the
storyline for poems that sprout from nature's legacy of winter
snow or spring blossoms is a customary ritual blend for poets
who indulge in the art of the imagination. Even under
lockdown, the wings of the imagination can soar and prosper
giving rise to a new set of poems each month no matter what
the season.

ISBN: 9798504464992 • $24.95
Available through Amazon.com

JUNE 7

Oh, the sound is gone
In my computer.
My bags are packed
How is it in a single day
Rome was sacked.

JUNE 1

How could you think that way?
All that is lovely must go into the dust?
All that is lonely must go into the dust.
You've got to create the illusion
That time does not matter
But it does and so it must!

Hearing the Cries of the World

We may have plenty of time in order to try to understand our human insignificance as cosmic raindrops adrift on the sea of life. Calendars are one way of keeping track of signs. Each poem may be a welcome sign pointing to a path honoring our faith so that we can now discover a choreographed trajectory, a way filled with particles mediating and radiating an inner gospel of light.

The seasons wheel on until we see face to face through a glass darkly. Is every act of breathing part of global warming? The presence of other people's voices in our experience as charted in these poems may help us to soldier on. We are waiting for calendars to define who we are as reflected in parables of light years.

ISBN 9798791430953 • $24.95
Available through Amazon.com

Moon in Taurus

Representing her newest collection, these poems by Elizabeth Bishop center on familiar themes of loss, grief, and also the gaining of a new astrological perspective. Within this collection, astrology serves as a metaphorical trope that communicates a reassuring intimacy awash with planetary configurations.

Navigating the way poets envision the life of an artist is what some of these poems are about. One can sense a comedic underpinning and wry overtones of a back story. Under the daring guidance of several mentors, Bishop's work is always changing in order to meet the contemporary aesthetic exigencies of the craft. Written over a six month period in 2021, these poems reflect the challenging yet vibrant textures of an elder.

ISBN: 9798418965837
Available through Amazon.com

ELIZABETH MARTINA BISHOP

The Inner Eye of Reason

Poems written at the end of the pandemic. Will the pandemic come back? Will everything remain the same as it once was before? Nothing is the same except the recycling of historical patterns captured in poetry. The voice of reason may hold out. Or, it may not.

The logic of poetry extends over time and space. Choose a poem for your birthday; read it aloud in order to seek the recurring presence of rhyme or reason to match the psyche's quixotic quest for a dreamer's cosmos. Reading poems may awaken the irreverent logic of the dreamer, within and without.

Poetry may harmonize with memories of happier days. Poetry may offer and gift you with a ray of hope as you travel through this topsy turvy world without fear.

ISBN: 9798444554289
Available through Amazon.com

At the Foot of the Mountain

This book represents a miscellaneous compendium of poems by Elizabeth Martina Bishop. Some of the poems were written when she took a class from one of her former Navajo students. The poems include some prose poems and some responses to specific writing prompts.

The collection includes poems indicative of a wide-ranging variety of style, form, and craft and indicates the different ways poems can come swimming into print. While the sources of inspiration may differ, poetry comes to Elizabeth in a multiplicity of vignettes which she is now eager to share with you, the reader.

ISBN: 9798802925058
Available through Amazon.com

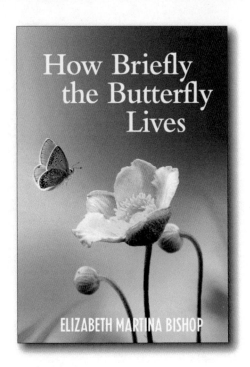

How Briefly the Butterfly Lives

You see the butterfly
on the front cover
and know life is brief
and the life
of every poem
also is very brief...

ISBN: 9798370554902
Available through Amazon.com

CHILDREN'S BOOKS

In this section, readers will find a wide variety of children's books suitable for many different ages.These books reflect the author's interest in indigenous wisdom stories. Many of the stories pertain to Snowflake the Magic Cat, which is part of a series. Other stories pertain to animal wisdom stories such as those found among the challenging adventures of other animals such as: quail, lynx, dogs, as well as birds. All of the stories contain some teaching wisdom tales and often feature Sedona's red rocks as the central landscape.

Attractive illustrations by Victoria O'Neill contribute greatly to the author's storyline.

Snowflake the Magic Cat

Snowflake the Magic Cat has a curious effect on people's dreams, causing them to have all kinds of life changing experiences.

Beautifully illustrated, this is the author's first children's book.

ISBN: 978-1982094843 $9.95
Available through Amazon.com

Magic Cat Meets Magic Dog

This book shows a meeting taking place between Snowflake, a cat and Bianca Teacup, a Pomeranian Dog.

One day, Sonia and Snowflake go into Sedona and discover a new crystal shop.

At first hesitant to make new friends, Sonia and Snowflake cannot believe their eyes when they experience a surprise.

At a nearby crystal shop, the two discover a tiny Pomeranian dog asleep inside a woven basket filled with beautiful amethysts. Why has this dog been left alone in the crystal shop? To whom does he really belong? Where is his owner?

At first, Sonia and Snowflake plot to hold up a sign stating the Pomeranian has been lost. They offer a reward for anyone who can find his owner. Suddenly, an elderly, grey- haired woman appears and claims the dog as her very own.

The new friends then proceed down the road as they become joyful and grateful about their new friends as well as their serendipitous meeting. They also enjoy the red rocks of Sedona.

ISBN: 9781729814383 $9.95
Available through Amazon.com

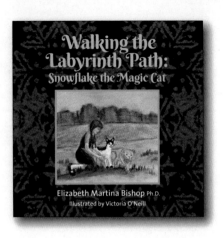

Walking the Labyrinth Path

Walking the Labyrinth Path details poignant adventure stories about Snowflake and Sophia and is the third book in a trilogy. The other two books include: *Snowflake the Magic Cat,* and *Magic Cat Meets Magic Dog.*

In this imaginative children's book, Snowflake and Sophia set out on a big adventure to find Wisdom Lake. During Autumn's changing landscape, Sophia and Snowflake experience the many wonders of nature and demonstrate how compassionate human beings can learn from animals and vice versa.

While learning about how to walk a labyrinth, the two friends also rescue a baby mountain lion. With inspiring and beautiful pictures by illustrator, Victoria O'Neill, the inspiring friendship between Sophia and Snowflake deepens and comes alive transporting readers to poetic realms

ISBN: 9781697186697 $9.95
Available through Amazon.com

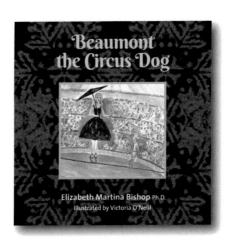

Beaumont
the Circus Dog

From pampered poodle in a New York City brownstone apartment to a circus dog in Paris. This book traces the history of an imaginary poodle named Beaumont who is taken to Paris by a butler and taught circus tricks so he can join a vaudeville circus troupe and entertain audiences by walking the tightrope in his magical pink toe shoes. Paddie is a man who helps

Beaumont achieves his dreams of stardom. In helping Beaumont realize and celebrate a new way of life, Paddie himself finds peace and contentment as Beaumont's new master.

ISBN:9798623137043 $9.95
Available through Amazon.com

Benny, the Little Quail Arrives at the Truth

Benny is a little quail who, despite his miniature size, fosters big dreams. Despite the fact, he wants to go for a balloon ride and see Paris, Benny doesn't really understand how to fly as high as the clouds in the sky. No matter what, though, Benny remains rather keen to find a way to see Mother Earth from a distance. Born in the rugged terrain of the Sedona Desert, Benny is not sure how to stretch his little wings and gain some altitude whereby his big dreams can be met on a grand scale. One day,

Benny sees some kittens playing in a nearby arroyo; he believes they might become fast friends. Soon something happens that serves to spur the story forward. Benny and feline family members glimpse an advertisement for a local balloon ride.Later, kitten and quail parents put their heads together and plan a surprise outing for the two families. After the balloon ride, both kittens and quail enjoy a new and unexpected bond of friendship. While Paris may not have been included in the balloon ride, both families have enjoyed seeing the sights of the Sedona community from a unique perspective.

ISBN:9798623137043 $9.95
Available through Amazon.com

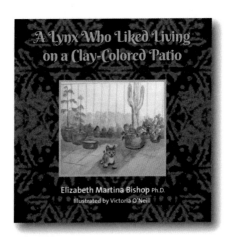

A Lynx Who Liked Living on a Clay-Colored Patio

No one could predict what would happen when a young family of lynxes (bobcats) decided to make their home on a patio normally frequented by humans. An entire story was revealed featuring a cooling tub of water and a nice place to cool down in the shade. Mr. Coyote never thought he had met his match when he tried to get into the picture.

The patio did not welcome his intrusion and he was sent back down into the arroyo. A riveting teaching tale with plenty of wisdom stories tucked within that will help take up the summer reading term. Geared for ages 6-10, young readers will learn about some of the life-saving habits of lynxes and acts of compassion.

ISBN: ISBN: 9798725092356 $9.95
Available through Amazon.com

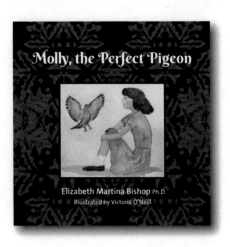

Molly, the Perfect Pigeon

A little girl named Tasha is having a hard time in school. She feels like she belongs in nature. In fact, she spends a lot of her time daydreaming about clouds, rocks, animals, and stars. One day Tasha meets a gate-keeper and a story-teller Molly, a creature known as the perfect pigeon. Molly is well-known in the community as a pigeon that knows many wisdom stories and often passes them down from one generation to another.

By chance, while Tasha is playing truant and trying to escape from recurrent bouts of boredom at her local school, she happens to meet Molly. Tasha's life begins to change in a very subtle manner. The location of Molly's nest in an abandoned schoolyard right next door to Tasha's school is what makes the meetings between bird and human possible. An immediate friendship develops.

ISBN: 9798453345847 $9.95
Available through Amazon.com

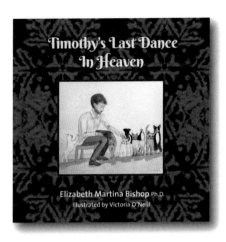

Timothy's Last Dance In Heaven

Timothy loves cats and folk dancing. Nina loves cats. She has a magical cat named Snowflake. One day Timothy has an accident and falls off his bike. In the middle of his falling he slips into a dream state and dreams of a magical cat named Snowflake. He goes through a tunnel and sees himself dancing with all kinds of cats.

Nina wishes her cat to never leave her. Timothy realizes that his dream is filled with lovely cats all folk dancing which he loves to do. When Nina wakes up from her dream, she finds her cat sitting on her book. As she reads the book, she finds a story about Timothy's dreaming.

She wonders if all of life is but a dream.

She realizes her cat is more than just an ordinary cat, because Snowflake is filled with magical surprises and he is able to make her feel protected.

Timothy realizes that even though he had an accident, he also believes if he hadn't had an accident, he never would have experienced such a lovely dream!

ISBN: ISBN: 9798490454649 • $9.95
Available through Amazon.com

REVIEWS

REVIEW

Selected Poems 1987-2015

Elizabeth Bishop and I discovered our connections as soul sisters at the Albuquerque SEED conference on Original Thinking. We planted our seeds by exchanging our poems. As an artist and founder of Living Labyrinths for Peace, I write this review to give deep thanks for her inspiring contribution to all of us.

In the chapters of the "Selected Poems," Elizabeth creates spiritual or mystical poems which inspire meditation. She uses such archetypes as: 1.) The Darkness and the Light 2.) The Mandala and the Labyrinth 3.) Cycles 4.) Elements, and 5.) The Dance.

Elizabeth honors all forms of spirituality such as Sufi, Buddhist, and Native American Shamanism as seen in "Mud Palace of Aberdeen." She encourages our day and night dreams, inspiring the healing of the inner heart and the one heart. In her poem "Transformation," she says: "I will not compete against myself or anyone else." She relates to nature as a form of meditation: i.e. "Ode to a Bear," "Mother Spider," and for environmental causes: "Wind Rushing through the Trees." She believes in the power of woman's spirituality: "Poetry is a way of integrating 'herstory' as well as 'history.'"

The light and dark are one: "Poetry mediates the inner realms, implementing the shameless interplay between light and dark." Life is a Labyrinth Dance that integrates the elements of earth (body), water (emotions), fire (mind) and spirit (air) through the cycles of Birth, Life, Death and Rebirth.

Her images and language—free verse, lyric works, formal sonnets and poems, and surrealist type poems—integrate the arts: She says: "Music, dance, video and poetry are one. Poetry should be sung." Her subjects and archetypes are all spiritually involving everyone through meditation to find their own answers: In "Radio Show: Poetic Soul's Remembrances," she says: "What the poem was about is anyone's guess. Children responded in their own words." I respond by bringing my own words through my poems, which connect with hers.

Sandra Wasko-Flood

Stonehenge Blues

*Upon reading Stonehenge Blues, I realize that the subject
matter is not so much about Stonehenge per se (I did not find
mere mention of the stones), but Bishop's perspectives on a
monolithic theme: say, the family "Bible". For instance:
"Tragedy always befalls one on the road to creation."*

*First there is the story of Pumpkin, and all her relations, told
via segments of prose, letters, and verse. About halfway through
it seems that Pumpkin is none other than the poet, Bishop,
when parallel lives cross and the first person pronoun takes
precedence. Poetic forms, too, become hazy as prose becomes
poetry and poetry, prose. Said in another way: what was once
an ominous Judge becomes a string of personal reflections, tarot
interpretations, divinations, and conversations. "What I have
for you are poems. Love poems, spoken, whispered, half-told
stories."*

*Somewhere between Ireland, Scotland, Louisiana, Boston,
Boulder, the Grand Canyon State, and Queens: "Is she a
prophet, a seer, or a gambler? / The odds of predicting
inclement weather are 50/50.*

Steven R. A. Johnson

My Feet Talk to the Road

This book of poetry and prose is largely a work of divination, on Tarot in particular, that doubles as an instruction manual for the metaphysically challenged. I'm not sure that I'll reach 8th chakra awareness and go on to recall past lives, or prophesy future lives; nevertheless, the work is written in a language that facilities dreaming, and it seems dreamtime is the stuff these poems/stories/characters are made of. How to distinguish bloodlines of the soul from those of ancestry, and what to do when the two come together? Second-generation travellers act as stand-in scholars in a culture where language blows in the wind. The stories and readings are multi-dimensional forgeries including stage notes and ceremony, poetical incantations. Well worth buying, especially for its glossary of terms from a seldom-annotated traveller's language, the Celtic shelte. A highly synchronistic read.

Steven R. A. Johnson

Wind Rushing through a Nest of Stars

Particularly poignant in these times, Wind Rushing Through a Nest of Stars embodies the juxtaposition of humanity with nature—that is, as one. Reed marshes, the fox, Mother Spider, the ghost of winter are integrated into our everyday (and not so everyday) human experience. The prose poems, stories, and poems offer multifaceted perspectives, such as historic, contemporary, otherworldly, political, like a Picasso painting bringing forth a unique view of the whole. Bishop's commentaries not only pertain to environmental issues but also encompass the many other concerns incurred as a result of modern, industrial globalization. While offering a candid narrative of this course and its consequences, the poems and stories continue to remind us of the connection we have to the more than human world.

Astrid Berg

REVIEW

Soulmate in a Kayak

A collection of four loosely fitting vignettes, Soulmate in a Kayak reads like a waking dream. Bishop explores the function and purpose of the serene, confounding, stinging chatter of the mind and reflects on the isolation, humor, and meaningfulness felt while searching for purpose. Living on the periphery of the collective requires a willingness to inhabit our contradictions and unplumbed depths. Should one feel shame for pondering the possibility of existing in multiple worlds? Perhaps some meaning is found in posing the question of purpose? Could nature itself have a soul? When one tries to pierce the veil of nothingness through mediation why does it often only lead to a cramp in the neck? Have humans lost the ability to understand ourselves and our role? What have we lost that was once accessible to our elders and how will we know what it was if we find it? These are several of the overlapping themes explored in the early pages of Soulmate in a Kayak.

Later Bishop artfully adds Love to the mix. When finding one's soulmate--like a diamond in the rough--what are we losing when the relationship becomes more smoothly faceted? With the wisdom of age our cynicism from past experience taints the possibility of a pure love. Do we want to forget this and risk reopening ourselves to disappointment and suffering? To experience life, love, and purpose Bishop's prose suggests that we need to allow ourselves to often exist in a vulnerable state.

Soulmate in a Kayak is a book that you'll want to keep close. It is a book to sip and ponder. Let Elizabeth Martina Bishop hold your hand then let it go. You are free to wander along a place of wonder.

Luke Kettle

Black Swan

The prose poems are graceful and engage the reader through an inquisitive tone. Perhaps this is the method of the black swan in society, the one who appears in the pub or hostel and asks those questions that, in themselves, reveal the threads that weave through lifetimes of kindred souls and ironic caricatures. The work is poetic: things as symbols take great precedence over any kind of idea or conception of the poet. These are poems for gypsies and those who take delight in choosing the wrong card from a tarot deck. Gossip is at the level of the birds. Biodiversity in this poetry cuts through the narrow economies of human sentimentality and reveals the absurdity of love itself all wrapped up in the image of the artist. The poems are easy to read, but I'd recommend keeping an OED handy for the occasionally exquisite term that pops up from antiquity.

Steven R. A. Johnson

Cosmic Excuse

Great poetry, an uplifting reading experience. Elizabeth Bishop's poems sport tones of new age spirituality, myth, and ancestral musings all kept in check with a healthy dose of irony and irreverence. Ego might dissolve into one's personal totem displayed on the page. Love and sorrow; tryst, trust, loss; the mystery of impermanence within this precious human life read like prayers in the wind. These poems will appear again and again: just as they have in the past, so too will they appear in lifetimes beyond this one. Thus, the poet has perspective.

Steven R. A. Johnson

The Mud Palace of Aberdeen

Some long and divinatory prose poems, some sweet and lyrical pieces of meaningful, melopoeic associations. "Divination takes place only on certain days when the moon agrees not to be mars." Sometimes I am lost in the ether of space poetry, at others I am brought back by shamanistic verses that can't help but command emptiness, space, the immediate surrounds. Dervishes, rainbows, caravans, prophets, seers: all kinds of poems weave a magical net of ancestry and spirit. Women make much of time in tidbits of intergenerational irony. A secret autobiography is revealed as a grandmother spirit in a flask. The lifetime of one solitary seer becomes the singular thought of an ordinary being while the emotional injustices of an ordinary being are enveloped in remembrance of the poet's sense of grace. The back cover claims: "A whirlwind tour of Native American shamanism. Or just plain shamanism." I didn't really get more than one or two explicit references to Native Americans—mostly just the impression that good "Western" medicine is humility.

Steven R. A. Johnson

As Long As We Both Shall Dance

"Powerful, impenitent, shameless"

Either from an unimpeded perspective of the archetype itself or a candid tarot reading, you experience the 22 symbols in the major arcana of the tarot. In their expressions, the archetypes remind me of the Greek or Roman pantheon— powerful, impenitent, shameless and fully themselves. The readings are not rose-colored, but interpretations filled with the grittiness of real life. Each it's own story and some continuations that, by depicting the background and temperament of the person seeking advice, exposes our characteristic humane frailties. This is not a book for those seeking a clear explanation of symbolic meanings or a how-to of the Tarot. Instead, Bishop skillfully weaves together fragments of images, sensations and dialogue to offer dreamtime impressions, not explanations. Hence you are left with a knowing that goes deeper than what you cognitive self can grasp.

Astrid Berg

Made in the USA
Las Vegas, NV
19 June 2023

73550627R00093